Papa Love

The Story of True Love

Illustrated and written by
Nolly Mercado

Nolly Mercado

Tellwell Talent
www.tellwell.ca

ISBN
978-1-77370-174-5 (Hardcover)
978-1-77370-173-8 (Paperback)

PART 1:
The Beginning

In the beginning, before everything else was created, there was Papa Love, and he was pure love. Papa Love is God and he is the father of everyone.

Papa Love had a son named Jesus, and together they lived with Holy Spirit.

Papa Love is very creative. His biggest dream was to create many kids that looked like him, into whom he could pour out his love. His first children were Adam and Eve. He also created a big garden for all of them to live in and enjoy their life together with him. Their hearts were full of his love.

Inside the garden, there was a very unique tree. Papa Love asked Adam and Eve not to eat its fruit because it would make it difficult for them to hear and see him. They made a wrong choice by eating from the tree. Sadly, they had to leave the beautiful garden Papa Love created for them.

When Papa Love learned what they had done he called out to them, but they were afraid that he would be angry at them and they hid from him. Papa Love was heartbroken because he had lost his children. Nevertheless, he kept loving them.

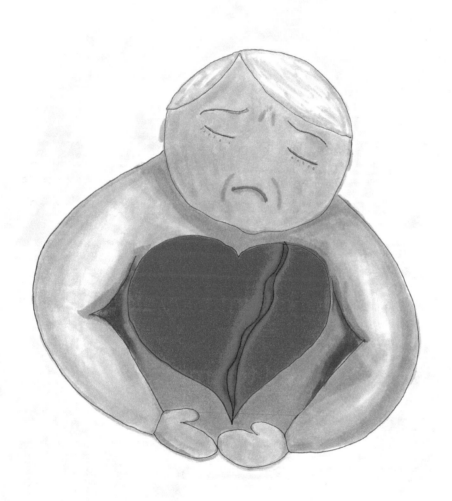

Papa Love and Jesus loved each other very deeply. When Jesus saw Papa Love was sad, he offered himself to come to Earth to go find his children. Jesus and Papa Love got together with Holy Spirit to make a plan.

Jesus was very excited to embrace the most marvelous adventure that had ever happened on Earth. It was one motivated by true love.

PART 2:
Love Comes Down

The first part of the plan was to bring Jesus into Earth. Holy Spirit put baby Jesus into the womb of a young woman named Mary, so he could be born on Earth, just like the rest of us.

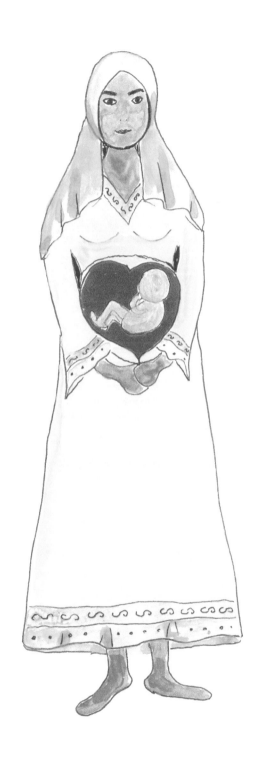

Jesus was human like his mom, and God, like his dad. Jesus' mission on earth was to let us know the truth about who we belong to, who our real father is and how much we are loved by him.

Papa Love lived in Jesus' heart. Jesus did and said only what Papa Love told him to, so everyone who met Jesus met Papa Love too. And he did a very good job.

As part of the plan, Jesus had to die on a cross. This moment was heartbreaking for Papa Love. He wanted to come down to Earth to release his son from that horrible cross, and Jesus wanted to step down from there too. But they both endured that moment to bring Papa's forgiveness to all. Now everyone could start a new relationship with Papa as it was in the beginning.

Jesus is the only way to Papa Love.

After that, Jesus returned home, and he is now sitting in Papa Love's lap.

As a gift, he also made it possible for Holy Spirit to enter into our hearts and fill them with his love. Holy Spirit is now our direct line to hear and see Papa Love from Earth.

PART 3:
You & Papa Love

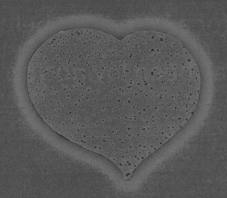

Papa Love's dream was to have many children to share his love with. You were as small as one of these dots in his heart and you lived there for a long time before you were born. He has been loving you since then.

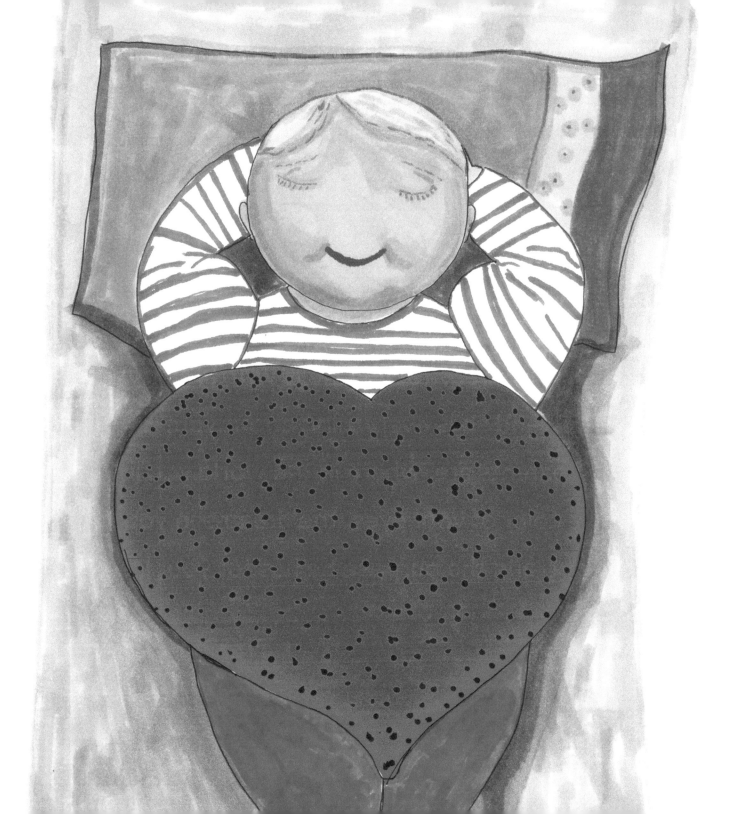

Papa Love has a special book where he writes everything there is to know about each one of his children. Your name is written in that book, and so is everything about you: who your parents are, where in the world you live, the color of your eyes, the dreams in your heart, and the purpose he has for your life.

Papa Love was with you in your mother's womb and he received you when you were born. You are perfectly and wonderfully made. His love for you is unique and he does not share it with anyone else.

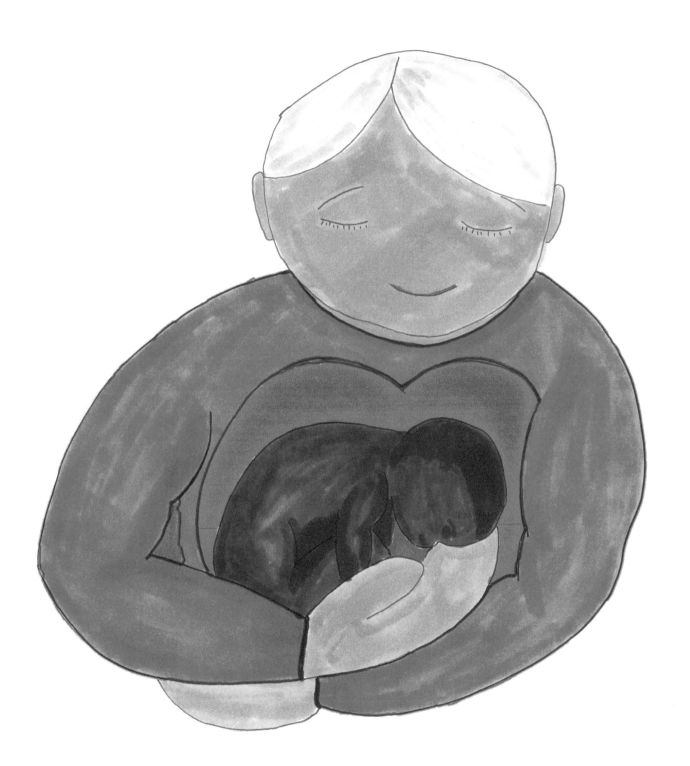

Jesus wants to be your true friend. If you invite him into your heart, he will come with Papa Love and Holy Spirit and they will build a house there and live with you forever. You will never be alone.

When Papa Love, Jesus, and Holy Spirit live inside your heart, you can talk to them any time, just like you talk to your best friend.

Papa Love has a huge amount of love to fill up your heart. When you feel cranky, mad, or sad you just have to call out to him and ask him to give you more of his love.

When your heart is filled with his love, you feel joy and happiness, no matter what is going on around you. His love, in turn, makes you want to love everyone around you.

Papa Love delights in you and he sings

songs of love over you to calm your fears.

His love always protects you.

Papa Love's dream came true because of what Jesus did on the cross. Now he lives in your heart, and you and Jesus live in his, forever; nothing could ever separate you from his love.

He is loving you right now!

CPSIA information can be obtained
at www.ICGtesting.com
Printed in the USA
LVHW01n1019081217
559101LV00002B/8/P